A GIFT FOR

Mrs. Sherrie Brown

FROM

The Smiths ♥ Brandon Shurrell
Kendall & Kaleb

DATE

February 20, 2016

All of Our Love
~Today Tomorrow & Always

IF GOD WROTE YOUR

Birthday Card

A CELEBRATION OF YOU FROM THE ONE WHO KNOWS YOU BEST

IMAGINED BY

JAY PAYLEITNER

Ellie Claire™ Gift & Paper
Brentwood, TN 37027
EllieClaire.com

If God Wrote Your Birthday Card
© 2013 by Jay Payleitner
Published by Ellie Claire, an imprint of Worthy Media, Inc.

ISBN 978-1-60936-837-1

Stock or custom editions of Ellie Claire titles may be purchased in bulk for educational,
business, ministry, fundraising, or sales promotional use. For information, please e-mail info@
EllieClaire.com.

Cover photo © iStockphoto

Cover and interior design by Greg Jackson | ThinkPen.com

Printed in China

1 2 3 4 5 6 7 8 9 – 18 17 16 15 14 13

Dedicated with love
to my mom on her eighty-sixth birthday
and my grandson, Jackson, on his first.

THERE IS NOT ENOUGH DARKNESS
IN ALL THE WORLD
TO PUT OUT THE LIGHT OF
EVEN THE SMALLEST CANDLE.

ROBERT ALDEN

IMAGINE

Imagine the Creator of the Universe slipping into the back of the room at your birthday party. *You didn't even think to invite Him.* But He loves you so much that He crashes your party. Really, He just wants to make sure your birthday and this coming year are the best ever.

Suddenly, the lights go off and a cake is carried into the room. Flickering candles surround your name in icing and reflect off the faces of all the people who care so much about you. They even sing a song in your honor.

You look around, a little embarrassed. But a gentle smile from the One across the room reminds you today is your day. And you are worthy of a little extra attention.

Someone says, "Make a wish!" So you pause and imagine all the things you ever wanted to have, ever wanted to do, and ever wanted to be.

You close your eyes. Tight. And you wish.

But the One who knows everything about you already knows your wish.

With one breath you blow out every candle. And a fresh new year officially arrives.

As the last guest leaves, you plop into a chair. And notice an envelope still unopened. Gently you slide out the card and let the words speak to you. The card brings perspective for yesterday, cheers for today, and promises for tomorrow. Amazingly, it's signed by the One who loves you most.

To be sure, the contents of that birthday card recorded in these pages are inspired. We know the words are prophetic and revelational because they are restatements of truths found in Scripture. The footnotes that accompany each passage reference back to biblical text.

Read it for yourself. As you turn theses pages, remember this is not a generic message by an unknown writer you will never meet. Trust that every word of this love letter has been written specifically for you. Like the Bible itself, these promises are meant to be taken very personally.

This is a

wonderful day.

This is the day the Lord has made.
We will rejoice and be glad in it.

PSALM 118:24

A day to

celebrate you.

I have loved you with an everlasting love.

JEREMIAH 31:3 NIV

My child, I've been anticipating this da

forever.

I've known you since before you were born.

I knew you before I formed you in your mother's womb.
Before you were born I set you apart.

JEREMIAH 1:5

You were no small task

ith love and care,

I crafted every amazing detail of who you are.

I praise you because I am fearfully and wonderfully made;
your works are wonderful, I know that full well. My frame
was not hidden from you when I was made in the secret place,
when I was woven together in the depths of the earth.

PSALM 139:14–15 NIV

Your image is carved

on the palm
of my hand.

I will not forget you! See, I have engraved you on the palms of my hands.
ISAIAH 49:15–16 NIV

Every minute of your life

precious to Me.

Every day of my life was recorded in your book. Every moment
was laid out before a single day had passed.

PSALM 139:16

The plans I have for yo

are beyond your imagination.

And beyond the imagination of anyone who ever lived.

For since the world began, no ear has heard and no eye has seen a God like you, who works for those who wait for him!

ISAIAH 64:4

I gave you

unique gifts.

God has given each of you a gift from his great variety of
spiritual gifts. Use them well to serve one another.

1 PETER 4:10

I gave you

unique tasks.

Do you have the gift of speaking? Then speak as though God himself were speaking through you. Do you have the gift of helping others? Do it with all the strength and energy that God supplies.

1 PETER 4:11

I want you to shine brightl

ecause, dear child,

you make Me
smile.

The Lord directs the steps of the godly.
He delights in every detail of their lives.

PSALM 37:23

When I look at you

I see Myself reflected in your face.

So all of us who have had that veil removed can see and reflect the glory of the Lord. And the Lord—who is the Spirit—makes us more and more like him as we are changed into his glorious image.

2 CORINTHIANS 3:18

You may be surprised to hear
that I endorse the time-honored
tradition of making a wish

just before you blow out birthday candles. I am, after all, in the business of

listening carefully and granting wishes generously.

If you remain in me and my words remain in you,
ask whatever you wish, and it will be done for you.
JOHN 15:7 NIV

Often you'll receive exactly
what you wish for.

But when your long-term vision isn't quite clear, I might overrule your wish. That's part of My promise to protect and provide for you.

God's way is perfect. All the LORD's promises prove true.
He is a shield for all who look to him for protection.

PSALM 18:30

Some people don't like birthdays
Especially the counting part

But reflecting on the arc of your life will give you **a much-needed perspective.**

Teach us to number our days, that we may gain a heart of wisdom.
PSALM 90:12 NIV

Birthdays can also remind you that there

a beginning and an end
to your time on earth.

LORD, remind me how brief my time on earth will be.
Remind me that my days are numbered—how fleeting my life is.

PSALM 39:4

So make the most of your day

...ot wasting time with stuff that doesn't matter or doesn't last.

So be careful how you live. Don't live like fools, but like those who are wise. Make the most of every opportunity in these evil days.

EPHESIANS 5:15–16

I also love birthdays

ecause they are a great excuse
for acting like a kid
again. And that's a good thing.

And he said: "Truly I tell you, unless you change and become like
little children, you will never enter the kingdom of heaven."

MATTHEW 18:3 NIV

My child

ou have My full

permission to party.

Not like the world parties.

When you follow the desires of your sinful nature, the results are very clear: sexual immorality, impurity, lustful pleasures, idolatry, sorcery, hostility, quarreling, jealousy, outbursts of anger, selfish ambition, dissension, division, envy, drunkenness, wild parties, and other sins like these.

GALATIANS 5:19–21

Instead, party like you've got

something to really celebrate

(Because you do.)

Praise God in his sanctuary; praise him in his mighty heaven! Praise him for his mighty works; praise his unequaled greatness! Praise him with a blast of the ram's horn; praise him with the lyre and harp! Praise him with the tambourine and dancing; praise him with strings and flutes! Praise him with a clash of cymbals; praise him with loud clanging cymbals. Let everything that breathes sing praises to the LORD!

PSALM 150:1–6

Party like you're overflowing

with love, joy, peace, patience, kindness, goodness, faithfulness, gentleness, and self-control.

The Holy Spirit produces this kind of fruit in our lives: love, joy, peace, patience, kindness, goodness, faithfulness, gentleness, and self-control.

GALATIANS 5:22–23

Party like

you're destined
for eternity.

Those who have been ransomed by the LORD will return. They will enter Jerusalem singing, crowned with everlasting joy. Sorrow and mourning will disappear, and they will be filled with joy and gladness.

ISAIAH 35:10

You may have notice

that this birthday card

does not include a big fat check.

There are practical reasons for that.

I am leaving you with a gift—peace of mind and heart. And the peace
I give is a gift the world cannot give. So don't be troubled or afraid.

JOHN 14:27

First, I am much more interested

n things that have

eternal value.

(Money is not one of those things.)

In the blink of an eye wealth disappears, for it will
sprout wings and fly away like an eagle.

PROVERBS 23:5

Second, worldly wealth becomes

a distraction from

what's really
important.

No one can serve two masters. For you will hate one and love the other;
you will be devoted to one and despise the other.
You cannot serve both God and money.

MATTHEW 6:24

As for wrapped presents

Are you disappointed because yo

dropped all kinds of hints and didn't ge

what you wanted? Or maybe you did get
exactly what you wanted and think
your life is now complete?

Wrong.
And wrong again.

Those who weep or who rejoice or who buy things should not be
absorbed by their weeping or their joy or their possessions.

1 CORINTHIANS 7:30

Stuff is overrated

Stuff doesn't last. Everything in this world —even the world itself—is temporary.

Those who use the things of the world should not become attached to them. For this world as we know it will soon pass away.

1 CORINTHIANS 7:31

Besides, if you invest your life in stuff

ou become a perfect target for Satan and miss **My plan for an extremely full life.**

The thief comes only to steal and kill and destroy; I came
that they may have life, and have it abundantly.

JOHN 10:10 NASB

My plan includes an invitation for you

to become a full-fledged member of My family —with all the privileges and benefits. How's that for a birthday surprise?

Now you are no longer a slave but God's own child.
And since you are his child, God has made you his heir.
GALATIANS 4:7

Funny thing about birthdays
most people don't want to be
the age they are

Kids want to be all grown up. Adults want to be kids again. But there are great benefits to every age.

The glory of the young is their strength; the gray hair of experience is the splendor of the old.

PROVERBS 20:29

To young people, I say enjoy your yout

This is a time of great discovery.

Push yourself. Train yourself to work hard.

It is good for people to submit at an early age to the yoke of his discipline.

LAMENTATIONS 3:27

You have much to offer

Don't let anyone tell you otherwise.

Don't let anyone think less of you because you are young.
Be an example to all believers in what you say, in the way
you live, in your love, your faith, and your purity.

1 TIMOTHY 4:12

You will make mistakes

nd there will be consequences.

Don't worry too much.

I've got your back.

Young people, it's wonderful to be young! Enjoy every minute of it.
Do everything you want to do; take it all in. But remember that
you must give an account to God for everything you do.

ECCLESIASTES 11:9

Still, even as you **dream big dream**
and think you're invincib

n't forget about Me. All your dreams, exuberance, and vitality are

My gift to you.

Don't let the excitement of youth cause you to forget
your Creator. Honor him in your youth before you grow old.
ECCLESIASTES 12:1

For anyone feeling old,

et Me confirm that you're not getting older,

you're getting better.

Gray hair is a crown of glory; it is gained by living a godly life.

PROVERBS 16:31

Your gathered wisdo

and experience have
earned you respect.

You shall rise up before the grayheaded and honor the aged.
LEVITICUS 19:32 NASB

74

You've done much.
But there's still much more to do.

Do not cast me off in the time of old age;
Do not forsake me when my strength fails.

PSALM 71:9 NASB

One of the great benefits
celebrating many birthda

s that you gain a valuable perspective.
For example, you begin to

see how I provide
for my children.

Once I was young, and now I am old. Yet I have never seen the
godly abandoned or their children begging for bread.

PSALM 37:25

And you finally

realize what matters

and what does not.

Is not wisdom found among the aged?
Does not long life bring understanding?

JOB 12:12 NIV

I am still your biggest fan

And I promise that

we're in this

together.

I will be your God throughout your lifetime—until your hair is white with age.
I made you, and I will care for you. I will carry you along and save you.

ISAIAH 46:4

No matter what your age may be

cherish every day.

When people live to be very old, let them rejoice in every day of life.

ECCLESIASTES 11:8

Between now and your next birthday

've got a year planned out
 you won't believe.

> No eye has seen, no ear has heard, and no mind has imagined
> what God has prepared for those who love him.
>
> 1 CORINTHIANS 2:9

To make the most of it

ou may need to do a little self-examination and personal housecleaning.

Examine yourselves to see if your faith is genuine. Test yourselves. Surely you know that Jesus Christ is among you; if not, you have failed the test of genuine faith.

2 CORINTHIANS 13:5

If you're carrying a burden

nload it right here.
Right now.

I can handle it.

Cast your cares on the LORD and he will sustain you;
he will never let the righteous be shaken.

PSALM 55:22 NIV

Feeling a little guilty over
past mistakes?

've already forgotten about them,
so you can let them go.

He has removed our sins as far from us as the east is from the west.
PSALM 103:12

Have a bad habit you'd like to break?

Helping people make a fresh start

is My favorite thing to do.

Do not conform to the pattern of this world, but be transformed by the renewing of your mind. Then you will be able to test and approve what God's will is—his good, pleasing and perfect will.

ROMANS 12:2 NIV

Carrying a grudge you'd like to get past

Let Me help you to forgive.

If you forgive those who sin against you, your heavenly Father will forgive you.
But if you refuse to forgive others, your Father will not forgive your sins.

MATTHEW 6:14–15

Feel like the world is passing you by
As if you're on the outside looking in

I've got a few secrets
to share with you.

Call to Me and I will answer you, and I will tell you great
and mighty things, which you do not know.

JEREMIAH 33:3 NASB

Need courage to face a giant?

I am bigger
than any challenge
you will ever confront.

This is my command—be strong and courageous! Do not be afraid or discouraged. For the LORD your God is with you wherever you go.

JOSHUA 1:9

Maybe you just need

a hug and some hope?

My arms will always be stretched open for you.

With a mighty hand and outstretched arm; His love endures forever

PSALM 136:12 NIV

My child, not just today, but every day,

ask Me. **Trust Me.** Everything you want and need can be yours. **Really.**

Therefore I say to you, all things for which you pray and ask, believe that you have received them, and they will be granted you.

MARK 11:24 NASB

So expect this coming year
to be **awesome**.

Expect **a well-marked path**
leading to a rewarding destination.

The LORD says, "I will guide you along the best pathway
for your life. I will advise you and watch over you."

PSALM 32:8

But even if you hit some bump

brambles, or snag

don't panic.
I'll be walking right beside you.

Each time he said, "My grace is all you need. My power works best in weakness." So now I am glad to boast about my weaknesses, so that the power of Christ can work through me.

2 CORINTHIANS 12:9

Choose to see the bright si

n every situation. What looks like a detour or setback **is really just more good news.**

When troubles come your way, consider it an opportunity for great joy. For you know that when your faith is tested, your endurance has a chance to grow. So let it grow, for when your endurance is fully developed, you will be perfect and complete, needing nothing.

JAMES 1:2–4

Indeed, every experience and relationship you have ever had comes together here and now.

You are ready for anything.

We know that in all things God works for the good of those who
love him, who have been called according to his purpose.

ROMANS 8:28 NIV

To recap.

You are worth celebrating.

A masterpiece created to do great things.

For we are God's masterpiece. He has created us anew in Christ Jesus, so we can do the good things he planned for us long ago.

EPHESIANS 2:10

Age is not an issue. Money is not an iss

Doubts, fears, questions, insecurities, and **past mistakes should never hold you back** from doing My work.

> May the favor of the Lord our God rest on us; establish the work
> of our hands for us—yes, establish the work of our hands.
>
> **PSALM 90:17 NIV**

So, if you are ready, here i

My two-part birthday challeng

to you. It's revolutionary. It's transformationa

It's world changin

1. Love.
2. Be loved.

1. Give love...
to Me.

Love the Lord your God with all your heart and with
all your soul and with all your mind.

MATTHEW 22:37 NIV

to others.

Love your neighbor as yourself.
MATTHEW 22:39 NIV

2. Accept love...
from Me.

> May you experience the love of Christ, though it is too great
> to understand fully. Then you will be made complete with all
> the fullness of life and power that comes from God.
>
> EPHESIANS 3:19

from others.

No one has ever seen God. But if we love each other, God lives
in us, and his love is brought to full expression in us.

1 JOHN 4:12

Is that something you can do?
Love Me?

Love every member of your family?
Love each and every friend?
Love each and every stranger?
Love each and every enemy?
And allow them to love you back?

You have heard the law that says, "Love your neighbor" and hate your enemy. But I say, love your enemies! Pray for those who persecute you! In that way, you will be acting as true children of your Father in heaven.

MATTHEW 5:43—45

Not as easy as you thought.
Right?

Don't just pretend to love others. Really love them.

ROMANS 12:9

My child, go for it. For the next twelve months, love like you have never loved before.

One year from now, don't be surprised at how much you have accomplished. Love works. Love conquers.

Love gives back.

Walk in the way of love, just as Christ loved us and gave himself up for us as a fragrant offering and sacrifice to God.

EPHESIANS 5:2 NIV

So that is my birthday gift to you:

My love.

And your ability to give and receive love.
It's the one gift that never fails.

Love is patient, love is kind. It does not envy, it does not boast, it is not proud. It does not dishonor others, it is not self-seeking, it is not easily angered, it keeps no record of wrongs. Love does not delight in evil but rejoices with the truth. It always protects, always trusts, always hopes, always perseveres. Love never fails.

1 CORINTHIANS 13:4–8 NIV

Scripture References

ABOUT THE AUTHOR

Jay Payleitner is a behind-the-scenes veteran of Christian radio, serving as producer for *Josh McDowell Radio, Jesus Freaks Radio, Project Angel Tree with Chuck Colson,* and *Today's Father* for The National Center for Fathering. Jay is also the best-selling author of *52 Things Kids Need from a Dad, 52 Things Wives Need from Their Husbands,* and *One-Minute Devotions for Dads,* and has been a guest on dozens of media outlets, including *Focus on the Family.* Jay and his high school sweetheart, Rita, make their home in the Chicago area where they've raised five great kids and loved on ten foster babies. You can read his weekly dadblog at jaypayleitner.com. Jay is also available to speak at men's events, parenting seminars, graduations, and…the occasional birthday party.

ALSO FROM JAY PAYLEITNER

Once Upon a Tandem

The One Year Life Verse Devotional

52 Things Kids Need from a Dad

365 Ways to Say "I Love You" to Your Kids

52 Things Wives Need from Their Husbands

52 Things Husbands Need from Their Wives

One-Minute Devotions for Dads

Do Something Beautiful

52 Things Daughters Need from Their Dads

52 Things Sons Need from Their Dads

If God Gave Your Graduation Speech

COUNT YOUR NIGHTS BY STARS,
NOT SHADOWS.

COUNT YOUR DAYS BY SMILES,
NOT TEARS.

AND ON ANY BIRTHDAY MORNING,

COUNT YOUR AGE BY FRIENDS,
NOT YEARS.